# Young Jesus

## By The McCormick Family

Published 2022 by Brent Tor Books

A loving grandmother had a dream of Jesus as a young boy. She shared her dream with her family, asking what would Jesus do, and together they created a book, *Young Jesus.*

This charming story takes readers into Young Jesus' childhood — playing with friends, helping his mother, fishing with his father, doing the kinds of activities every child identifies with. But Young Jesus was also connecting with his Heavenly Father as he prepared himself to become the Savior.

Children, parents, and grandparents will delight in the colorful depictions of the simple lessons Young Jesus learned that we all now know as the Gospel of Our Lord Jesus Christ.

YOUNG JESUS
Copyright © 2022 Brent Tor Books
BrentTorBooks.com

*Cover & Artwork*: All of the artwork within these pages are by Sophia and Matthew McCormick.

ISBN978-1-7337146-0-0

First Printing

All rights reserved. No part of the material may be reproduced in The United States of America or in any other country by any process, electronic or otherwise, in any material form or transmitted to any other person or stored electronically in any form without the prior written permission of the author.

The Catholic Edition of the Revised Standard Version of the Bible, copyright © 1965, 1966 National Council of the Churches of Christ in the United States of America. Used by permission. All rights reserved.

Book design: E.E.Weems

# Young Jesus

**Table of Contents**

1. Swimming Lesson
2. Not Ready
3. A Tree Climb
4. Scary Storms
5. Standing Strong
6. Family Outing
7. Young Helping Old
8. Alone and Brave
9. Dress Up Friends
10. Father's Will Be Done

# Chapter One: Swimming Lesson

**Young Jesus was impressed. "You are such a strong swimmer!" he yelled to his cousin John. "I want to be a strong swimmer."**

"Come swim with me, come swim with me," yelled John as he splashed through the water like a fish.

"Tell me how," said Young Jesus.

"Hold your breath, go all the way under, and push forward with your legs as hard as you can."

Young Jesus held his breath and dunked. Under the water he felt so different, an extra strength. He knew the water was a gift from God His Father, a gift that gave life to all the world. Breathless, Young Jesus leaped out of the water. He filled his lungs with air knowing that air was also a gift from God His Father that brought life to all the people on Earth.

Swimming was fun. It was his strength in the water and air, a celebration of the life and health God the Father had given to all the people on Earth.

Years later, before he was teaching, Jesus went to the Jordan River to be baptized by his cousin, John the Baptist, who had told so many people about the coming of the Savior. When he came out of the water, Jesus was filled with the Holy Spirit, the gift of life everlasting in Heaven.

*Matthew 3: 13-17 John Baptizes Jesus*

> *13 Then Jesus came from Galilee to John at the Jordan to be baptized by him. 14 And John tried to prevent Him, saying, "I need to be baptized by You, and are You coming to me?" 15 But Jesus answered and said to him, "Permit it to be so now, for thus it is fitting for us to fulfill all righteousness." Then he allowed Him. 16 When He had been baptized, Jesus came up immediately from the water; and behold, the heavens were opened to Him, and He saw the Spirit of God descending like a dove and alighting upon Him. 17 And suddenly a voice came from heaven, saying, "This is My beloved Son, in whom I am well pleased."*

# Chapter Two: Not Ready

**Young Jesus was unsure. "I don't think they're ready yet, Mother," he said. He was helping Mother Mary bake pistachio cakes for a special party.**

"Watch them carefully," she cautioned. "Don't let let them burn. We bake them golden brown and then drizzle them with honey."

"Can I pour the honey?" asked Young Jesus.

"Yes, but be careful and watch," Mother Mary reminded him. "You must bake them just right. Too soon and they will be raw, too long and they will be dry."

"Yes, Mother," said Young Jesus. And as he watched the pistachio cakes, he knew they would bake the exact amount of time necessary because God His Father would help him if he asked. "Please, Father," prayed Young Jesus, "help me bake them just right." And then as soon as he prayed, he knew his prayer would be answered.

"Oh, they are wonderful!" exclaimed Mother Mary when Jesus showed her the cakes. "You baked them so well, Jesus."

Years later, just before Jesus was teaching, he attended a wedding feast with Mother Mary. The wedding party ran out of wine, and Mother Mary asked Jesus to help the bride and groom. Even though he thought it wasn't yet his time, Mother Mary encouraged him to try, and then he performed his first miracle of changing the water into wine for the wedding feast.

*John 2: 3-10 Jesus Turns Water Into Wine*

> *3 When the wine was gone, Jesus' mother said to him, "They have no more wine." 4 "Woman, why do you involve me?" Jesus replied. "My hour has not yet come." 5 His mother said to the servants, "Do whatever he tells you." 6 Nearby stood six stone water jars, the kind used by the Jews for ceremonial washing, each holding from twenty to thirty gallons. 7 Jesus said to the servants, "Fill the jars with water;" so they filled them to the brim. 8 Then he told them, "Now draw some out and take it to the master of the banquet." They did so, 9 and the master of the banquet tasted the water that had been turned into wine. He did not realize where it had come from, though the servants who had drawn the water knew. Then he called the bridegroom aside 10 and said, "Everyone brings out the choice wine first and then the cheaper wine after the guests have had too much to drink; but you have saved the best till now."*

# Chapter Three: A Tree Climb

**Young Jesus was lonely. "There's no one to play with," he said.**

"Go find them," said Mother Mary. "Take some pistachios. If you find your friends, share your treat with them."

Young Jesus went down the lane. No one. Young Jesus went over the stone fence, into the sheep meadow. No one. Young Jesus saw a big tree, a fig tree. He knew it was God His Father's gift to the world. "I can climb that," he thought. "God will help me."

High, high, up he went, threading through the leafy branches. It was difficult to climb and a little scary being so high. But then from way up above, he was able to see his friends. They were in the far meadow, catching grasshoppers. Young Jesus climbed down and ran to help them.

Years later, when Jesus was teaching, a man named Zacchaeus climbed high up a fig tree for a clear view of him. Jesus saw him and remembered his scary tree climb when he was a boy. He knew how much Zacchaeus wanted to be saved. He knew God His Father had put that tree there as a gift for the world, and Zacchaeus had used that gift to prove that his faith in Jesus was stronger than his fear.

*Luke: 19: 1-6 Jesus Sees Zacchaeus*

> *1Jesus was passing through Jericho. 2 A man named Zacchaeus was there. He was the chief tax collector, and he was rich. 3 He tried to see who Jesus was. But Zacchaeus was a small man, and he couldn't see Jesus because of the crowd. 4 So Zacchaeus ran ahead and climbed a fig tree to see Jesus, who was coming that way. 5 When Jesus came to the tree, he looked up and said, "Zacchaeus, come down. I must stay at your house today." 6 Zacchaeus came down and was glad to welcome Jesus into his home.*

# Chapter Four: Scary Storms

**Young Jesus was frightened. "Father, the wind and the waves will sink our boat!"**

"I built this boat strong and sturdy," said Father Joseph. "It will not sink. Don't be afraid. Sit in the back while I row."

Young Jesus watched Father Joseph row the boat with great skill. The waves were big, the wind was fierce, but Young Jesus knew God His Father would never give Father Joseph more than he could handle.

They were drenched by the rain. They were pushed by the wind, but Father Joseph never stopped rowing. Young Jesus clapped when they reached shore. They were safe, and they still had plenty of fish to bring to Mother Mary to cook for supper.

Years later, when Jesus was teaching, he and his disciples were in a boat when a storm roared up. The disciples were fearful the boat would sink. Jesus wasn't afraid because he knew the wind and the waves were sent by God His Father to test their faith. He commanded the storm to calm itself, and it did.

*Mark 4: 37-41 Jesus Calms the Storm*

> *37 A furious squall came up, and the waves broke over the boat, so that it was nearly swamped. 38 Jesus was in the stern, sleeping on a cushion. The disciples woke him and said to him, "Teacher, don't you care if we drown?" 39 He got up, rebuked the wind and said to the waves, "Quiet! Be still!" Then the wind died down and it was completely calm. 40 He said to his disciples, "Why are you so afraid? Do you still have no faith?" 41 They were terrified and asked each other, "Who is this? Even the wind and the waves obey him!"*

# Chapter Five: Standing Strong

**Young Jesus was angry. "Stop that," he yelled.**

But the rough kids kept throwing mud balls at the back gate of the small synagogue in Nazareth. "Do not desecrate that holy place," Young Jesus told them.

The kids ignored him. Young Jesus watched as their mud balls splattered the temple wall. He could not allow them to do that. Young Jesus walked in front of them, and held up his hand. He knew God His Father would protect him if he stood strong. He was not afraid to face those kids. He was right, and they were wrong. "Go home, go home," he shouted. "Leave this place at once."

The rough kids, surprised by Young Jesus's determination, ran away. They would not fight him when they knew they were wrong.

Years later, when Jesus was teaching, he saw the money changers in the temple in Jerusalem. Once again he was angry that his father's house was being desecrated. He yelled and chased the money changers away. He knew it was the right thing to do because the house that God His Father gave to all people for worship should be respected above all other buildings.

*John 2: 14-16 Jesus Cleanses the Temple*

> *14 In the temple he found those who were selling oxen and sheep and pigeons, and the money-changers sitting there. 15 And making a whip of cords, he drove them all out of the temple, with the sheep and oxen. And he poured out the coins of the money-changers and overturned their tables. 16 And he told those who sold the pigeons, "Take these things away; do not make my Father's house a house of trade."*

# Chapter Six: Family Outing

**Young Jesus was confident. Mother Mary wanted to celebrate Father Joseph's birthday with a sunrise picnic at the beach, and Young Jesus was helping her make it an extra special day. He knew Father Joseph would be pleased.**

With Young Jesus' help, Mother Mary had cooked many delightful treats for them to eat. Young Jesus had packed their breakfast in a basket. And now he was carrying it to the beach near their house, where they could see the sunrise while Mother Mary and Father Joseph strolled hand in hand.

It was still dark in the early morning when they left their house for the long walk. Stars shone above and a full moon gave them light to walk the path. Young Jesus was content knowing that God His Father had created such a beautiful setting for their special day. It gave him confidence that their needs would always be met.

And then at the beach, as the amazing sun came up warm and bright, Young Jesus was so happy to share the beauty of a new day with his family. Father Joseph was delighted with his special birthday.

Years later, when he was teaching, Jesus was sharing God's word with thousands of people at a beach by the sea. When it grew late, his apostles warned him the multitude needed food. Jesus was confident that God His Father would provide for all. He blessed the small amount of bread and fish they had and passed it out to the crowd. Everyone ate. No one went hungry. There were baskets of leftovers. And all those people knew Jesus had performed a miracle.

*Matthew 14: 15-21 Jesus Feeds the Multitude*

> *15 When evening came, the disciples came to Him and said, "This is a remote and barren place, and the day is now over; send the throngs away into villages to buy food for themselves." 16 Jesus said: "They do not need to go away; you give them something to eat." 17 They said to Him, "We have nothing here but five loaves and two fish." 18 He said, "Bring them here to Me." 19 Then He ordered the crowds to recline on the grass; and he took the five loaves and two fish and looked up to heaven, He gave thanks and blessed and broke the loaves and handed the pieces to the disciples, and the disciples gave them to the people. 20 And they all ate and were satisfied. And they picked up twelve baskets full of the broken pieces left over. 21 And those who ate were about 5,000 men, not including women and children.*

# Chapter Seven: Young Helping Old

**Young Jesus was generous. "I filled your water jug. What else can I do for you?" he asked.**

"Thank you, Young Jesus, so much," said the old widow who lived in the small cottage at the edge of Galilee. "Drawing the water from the well is so hard for me now. You are so kind to do that for me."

"I can weed your garden," said Young Jesus, as he went into her garden and pulled the weeds. Then he took a broom and swept the dried leaves from her walkway.

After that, he offered to sweep out her house. "Oh, thank you, thank you," she said.

As he swept, Young Jesus saw how little the woman had in her one-room cottage. But he also saw her faith that God His Father had blessed her life. Simple furniture, simple kitchenware, just a small bit of food. But she was grateful and devout in her belief that she owed her thanks to God His Father.

Years later, when he was teaching, Jesus sat in the temple and watched how people donated to show their gratitude for God His Father. Wealthy men were showing off how much they gave. But when Jesus saw a widow donate a very small amount, he remembered how the widow he helped when he was a boy had lived so simply. He told his disciples the widow with her pennies was the most generous of the donors.

*Mark 12: 41-44 The Widow's Pennies*

> *41 Jesus sat down opposite the place where the offerings were put and watched the crowd putting their money into the temple treasury. Many rich people threw in large amounts. 42 But a poor widow came and put in two very small copper coins, worth only a few cents. 43 Calling his disciples to him, Jesus said, "Truly I tell you, this poor widow has put more into the treasury than all the others. 44 They all gave out of their wealth; but she, out of her poverty, put in everything—all she had to live on."*

# Chapter Eight: Alone and Brave

**Young Jesus was brave. He was alone, camping by the sea. He had built a fire and laid out his bedroll.**

Mother Mary and Father Joseph were not far away. But Jesus wanted to show them he was not a little boy anymore. He could camp by himself.

He had a water jug, some olives, and a loaf of bread. He had hoped to catch fish, but had no luck. Even though he was hungry, he knew he was strong enough to stay out all night by himself. It was a test he did not fear.

As he sat feeling hungry, he stopped worrying about food and looked at the beauty around him. He watched the birds and the tiny animals living within the bounty of nature. He inspected the wondrous insects God His Father had created. He knew he was part of the gift of life God had given all creatures, and it made him even more brave.

Years later, before he was teaching, Jesus fasted alone in the wilderness for forty days and forty nights. There, the devil tried to tempt him, but Jesus remembered how his solo campout had taught him to be brave. He sent the devil away without falling to temptation.

*Matthew 4: 1-11 Jesus Is Tested in the Wilderness*

> *4 Then Jesus was led by the Spirit into the wilderness to be tempted by the devil. 2 After fasting forty days and forty nights, he was hungry. 3 The tempter came to him and said, "If you are the Son of God, tell these stones to become bread." 4 Jesus answered, "It is written: 'Man shall not live on bread alone, but on every word that comes from the mouth of God.'" 5 Then the devil took him to the holy city and had him stand on the highest point of the temple. 6 "If you are the Son of God," he said, "throw yourself down. For it is written: "'He will command his angels concerning you, and they will lift you up in their hands, so that you will not strike your foot against a stone.'" 7 Jesus answered him, "It is also written: 'Do not put the Lord your God to the test.'" 8 Again, the devil took him to a very high mountain and showed him all the kingdoms of the world and their splendor. 9 "All this I will give you," he said, "if you will bow down and worship me." 10 Jesus said to him, "Away from me, Satan! For it is written: 'Worship the Lord your God, and serve him only.'" 11 Then the devil left him, and angels came and attended him.*

# Chapter Nine: Dress Up Friends

**Young Jesus was delighted. "Now you are the king," said his friend Young Bethany. "I've made you a crown of flowers."**

Young Jesus and Young Bethany were playing dress up. "Thank you," said Young Jesus, "I will wear your crown of flowers." And he smiled to himself because he knew that God His Father was the Creator of all kings and all flowers and all children at play.

Mother Mary and her friend Mother Sarah came to see the children's game. "Oh, Jesus," said Mother Sarah, "you are very kind and gentle to play dress up with Bethany."

"Bethany and I are friends," Young Jesus said. "It makes me happy when she makes me feel special."

Years later, when Jesus was teaching, he went to a dinner in a town called Bethany. During the dinner a woman named Mary came and washed his feet with her hair and anointed him with oil. Jesus remembered his friend Bethany and how pleased he was when she made him feel special.

*John 12: 2-7 Mary Washes Jesus Feet*

> *2 There they made Him a supper; and Martha served, but Lazarus was one of those who sat at the table with Him. 3 Then Mary took a pound of very costly oil of spikenard, anointed the feet of Jesus, and wiped His feet with her hair. And the house was filled with the fragrance of the oil. 4 But one of His disciples, Judas Iscariot, Simon's son, who would betray Him, said, 5 "Why was this fragrant oil not sold for three hundred denarii and given to the poor?" 6 This he said, not that he cared for the poor, but because he was a thief, and had the money box; and he used to take what was put in it. 7 But Jesus said, "Let her alone; she has kept this for the day of My burial. 8 For the poor you have with you always, but Me you do not have always."*

# Chapter Ten: Father's Will Be Done

**Young Jesus was exhausted. "I'm only halfway up the hill," he told himself.**

Young Jesus was helping Father Joseph with a carpentry job way at the top of a big hill. He was carrying boards up a steep path.

The boards were heavy and rough. He carried them on his back, and they cut his back through his tunic. But he did not hesitate or falter. Step after step, he carried the boards because Father Joseph had asked him to do this, and Jesus had promised he would.

Part of what made it hard was that he was alone. There was no one to help him, no one to encourage him. Young Jesus was hot and sweaty. He was thirsty and hungry. But he did not stop, because the higher he climbed, the more he felt he was also pleasing God His Father.

Finally, Young Jesus made it to the top with his heavy load. He smiled broadly as he set the wood down by his Father Joseph's workbench.

"Thank you, Jesus," said Father Joseph. "You have kept your promise to do this difficult task, and you have made me very proud."

Years later, when he had finished teaching all his earthly lessons, Jesus carried his cross up Calvary Hill where he was crucified. His final and most difficult task kept his promise and God the Father's promise that Jesus was the Savior.

*Matthew 16:24-26*

> *24 Then Jesus said to his disciples, "Whoever wants to be my disciple must deny themselves and take up their cross and follow me. 25 For whoever wants to save their life will lose it, but whoever loses their life for me will find it. 26 What good will it be for someone to gain the whole world, yet forfeit their soul? Or what can anyone give in exchange for their soul?"*